TELLING OUR BLUES WITH BLACK AMERICAN POETRY

Written By

Sharran C. Taylor

A.K.A. Poet Kween Yakini

Copyright © 2024, Telling Our Blues
Author, Sharran C. Taylor
Hookedonpoetry.com

All rights reserved. No part of this publication may be reproduced, distributed, or transmitted in any form by any means, including photocopying, recording, or other electronic methods without the prior written permission of the author, except in the case of brief quotations embodied in reviews and certain other noncommercial uses permitted by copyright law. For permission requests, email the author at *sharranctaylor00@gmail.com*

Portions of this book are works of fiction. Any references to historical events, real people, or real places have been used creatively by the author. Other names, characters, places, and events are products of the author's imagination, and any resemblances to actual events or places or persons, living or dead, are used artistically.

All rights reserved.

ISBN-13: 978-1-7323710-8-8

ISBN-10: 1732371088

Printed in the United States of America.

The Author's Note

What was it that made the Blues such a popular music genre? Was it the soulful down home sound, or was it the way it helped us tell our stories? Was it the way each note was sung, or was it the experiences that were being shared?

I love the Blues for all those reasons and more. The poet in me is especially drawn to the stories about real life experience that tapped into our own lives. I like the honesty, boldness, and audacity of Blues lyrics and how they were able to break the silence of heartbreak. And, like my ancestors before me, I wanted to use my voice to tell some new stories through the art of poetry. I want to leave behind my own creative scripts for the generations to come. My hope is that readers will find a story that they can connect with, and perhaps one day they too will share their stories.

TABLE OF CONTENTS

INTRODUCTION 1

WOMANLY BLUES

I'm a woman 3

She Stands In The Eye Of The Storm 10

A Black Gurl's Magic 14

The Majestic Headwrap 19

Aphrodesiac 25

Big, Black, & Beautiful 27

I Was Born A Queen 30

I See You, Sis 35

We Wear Crowns, Boo 41

Caught Up In The System 45

The Queen Protects The King 51

Goddess Within 57

THE OPEN MIC BLUES

If I Were A Poem	60
Mr. Poetry	66
I'll Tell You No Lie	72
I Only Date Sapiosexuals	79
Goddess On The Mic	87
A Rude Awakening	95
A Tree Without Roots	99
Poetic Bombshells	103

SOUL-SNATCHING BLUES

His Words	109
Sensual Symphony	112
Forget Me Not	116
He's Gone Now	119
My Kind Of Man	121
For A Season	124
The Treasure Of You	126
Sexual Demons	129

I Miss U	133
Do You Remember A Time?	138
Slightly Familiar Strangers	140
Here I Stand	142
Black Man They Will Never Love You Like I Love You	145

THE ANCESTRAL BLUES

A Place Called Point Comfort	150
Mrs. Tubman's Railroad	154
The Truth Of Sojourner	159
Her Name Was Sarah Baartman	163
A Message From Sarah Baartman	167
The Name Is Ida B. Wells	171
The Freedom Of Juneteenth	175
The Light Of Fannie Lou	184
The Day Rosa Sat Down	190
A Poem For Sandra	193
What Is Our Purpose?	200

INTRODUCTION

Black folks come from a long line of storytellers, and each generation has sought out the stories that shine the light on where we came from and who we really are. Storytelling is our way of saying "I am here, and I matter". We've learned the importance of sharing our voices and our experiences no matter if they be good or bad. Some of our deepest emotions and memories lay in between the spaces of the pages that we write on. Through the African Diaspora we have learned how to record our history by telling the stories that needed to be told by our Ancestors. Storytelling is how families were able to stay connected and it has reminded us of our roots. However, Black stories are often seasoned with pain, grit, relationship issues and personal battles that we sometime call the Blues. If you listen close to our stories, you just might hear the spirit of "Fannie Lou Hamer" and "Ida B. Wells" speaking.

WOMANLY BLUES

I'M A WOMAN

I'm a woman

I'm more powerful than you can imagine

My beauty goes deeper than you know

My DNA is infinite

So, ain't I a marvelous creation to behold?

Oh, but pardon me

Is my aura blinding you?

It seems this inner light that I carry

Just emanates from within

I guess that makes me

A grand sight for your sore eyes

I've been told that my smile is contagious

Some say that every freckle on my skin

Is a work of art

Although I am an acquired taste

As I can be too much for some

And not meant for everybody

'Cause I'm not a basic cup of tea

No, I'm more like a shot of warm brandy

I'm a woman!

From the top of my crown

To the bottom of my feet

I was made just as I should be

Beautiful inside and out!

After all

Glowing is what I'm about!

And I don't have to walk a mile in your shoes

To recognize your pain

Because I notice everything

I even noticed moment where you slipped

'Cause I've got that thing

What's that they call it?

Oh, yeah, "woman's intuition"

And believe me

That ain't nothing to play with

I'm a woman!

My DNA is a part of every man

Yet a man can only scratch my surface

I can be outspoken and demanding

But believe I'm worth it

Please don't get me wrong

I'm not trying to keep score

But whatever is given to me

I can probably multiply it by four

And my potential is too great

For me to be restricted or confined

So, honey, I don't waste my time

On those with insecure opinions

And narrow minds

Listen, I'm a woman

And I love me some me

My essence cannot be measured

I'm more than you can see

I have ambition in my blood

And royalty in my DNA

I'm self-driven and goal-oriented

'Cause I didn't come here to play

I'm a woman!

I've got more aspirations than I can count

And my to-do list never ends!

Honey, having me in your corner

Is like having a chef, a counselor,

A manager, and a best friend

'Cause I'm a natural healer

I'm soup for your soul

I'm that secret spice

In that New Orleans creole

Darling, if the world had no women

Tell me who would give birth

I don't care how cool you think you are Brotha

But it was a woman who knew you first

But when it's late at night

Some call me the night nurse

'Cause I'll send you to sleep on cloud nine

And have you wake up walking in reverse

I'm such a woman

That the word "beauty"

Can't even define me

And, if I may be totally honest,

I'm more like a goddess

Honey, I was made to be praised

I mean, look at all the sacrifices

And contributions I've made

So, you can say that I'm

Abundantly blessed

And I was made to bring forth life

So, I'm far from a damsel in distress

Plus, I'm a limited edition

Therefore, my time is priceless!

I'm a but you can also call me

The mother of civilization

Or call me an orator

Because my tongue has told the stories

Of many nations

Call me Eve

Because I'm the flower from the first garden

Call me a queen

Because I first wore the crown

Call me the backbone

Because I put the steel in your spine

Call me the original ancestor

Because I've been around since

The beginning of man kind

And I'm more powerful than you can imagine

And my beauty goes deeper than you know

My DNA is infinite

So, ain't I a marvelous creation to behold?

SHE STANDS IN THE EYE OF THE STORM

She's always been there

Fighting and standing by your side

Even when she was disregarded

By men who turned a blind eye

She's been the goddess of Earth

Since the beginning of mankind

She's your auntie

She's your sister

She's your ride or die

She's carried the world on her back

She stands in the eye of the storm

She's the origin of royalty

Ain't nothing about her the norm!

Haven't you noticed

The way she always has your back?

How she can see through your inner circle

And tell you where your enemies are at?

See how she uses the power of love

To conquer the negativity and hate

But she keeps everything 100

Because time is too precious to waste

Generation after generation

And time after time

She brings forth new life

'Cause she's a reflection of the divine

She's like Katherine Johnson

Who mastered the science of math

She carries the cure for diseases

Like the HeLa cells of Henrietta Lacks

She speaks truth like Angela Davis

And like Shirley Chisolm and Sister Betty

She's a revolutionary like Harriet Tubman

That's why she's always ready

She knows the power of music

Like the Blues of Billie and Nina

And no matter how much time has passed

We'll never forget Hurricane Katrina

She has the persistence of Serena and Venus

And she's as amazing as Simone Biles

She is Wilma Rudolph and Flo-Jo

Who always ran the extra mile

She's like the late Maya Angelou

She "knows why the cage bird sings"

And that's why she keeps rising

Like oppression ain't a thing!

So, remember, she's always been there

Standing right by your side

Even when she was disregarded

By men who turned a blind eye

She's been the goddess of Earth

Since the beginning of mankind

She's your auntie

She's your sister

She's your ride or die

A BLACK GURL'S MAGIC

Hey, you can go and tell it on the mountain!

Tell them that Black Gurls age

Like a fine wine

And that we were so loved by the creators

That they had to take their time!

And tell them that

When a Black Gurl is born

The stars appear to realign

Because we are so official

That even the Gods had to co-sign!

We have a natural resistance in our veins

And the magic is in our DNA

Our magnificence is so spectacular

That we'll take your breath away

Our skin tones are utterly exquisite

Our melanin is admired around the world

According to the trend on social media

It's lit to be a Black Gurl!

We got men losing their minds

For this melanin-rich pigment

But too much melanin

Can make a man act ignant

'Cause we got that

Rich, deep ebony with the light hazel eyes

And we got that butter pecan caramel

With them buttery thighs

We know y'all want the cocoa

With the smart and sexy combo

Body so snatched

You'll be paying for a condo

It's that dark blackberry

That makes us so extraordinary

We're too blessed to be stressed

And we're far from ordinary

We got that goddess effect

We shine from the inside out

And that's why folks still don't understand

What this Black gurl magic is about

'Cause our makeup stays flawless

And we be killing it in the streets

Looking like a Mary J. Blige

And we stay on fleek

We are often known for our

Beautiful full lips

And when it comes to that sass

We are fully equipped

This ancient beauty existed long before

Ebony, *Jet*, and *Essence* magazines

And it was definitely here before

That Covergirl and Maybelline

But if they could put this

Magic in a bottle

It would be the greatest

Treasure ever sold

But they better add

A pinch of the Caribbean

A dash of the Carolinas

And about a ½ cup of that

New Orleans Creole

We can be classy and elegant

Like Dianna Ross and the Supremes

But when a Black gurl comes for you

You'll be feeling like, "Dang, she's mean"

'Cause we ain't all made of

Sugar and Spice

And everything nice

Some of us are a little street

And a little hood

And we wish a mo-fo would!

So, you can go and tell it on the mountain!

Tell them that Black Gurls age

Like a fine wine

And that we were so loved by the creators

That they had to take their time!

And tell them that

When a Black Gurl is born

The stars appear to realign

Because we are so official

That even the Gods had to co-sign!

THE MAJESTIC HEADWRAP

Tell them that this isn't just some rag

We wear upon our heads

This is a majestic intertwining

Of vibrant colors and woven threads

This headwrap is a signal

That lets them other folks know

That the Black woman is a queen

Wherever she may go!

Allow me to enlighten you

On this part of Black history

'Cause it seems that our culture

Has become some type of mystery

I really want you to understand this

Allow me to give you the tea

Gather 'round family

Take a moment and sit with me

Listen, I don't know who needs to hear this

But Black hair has always been stigmatized

And because of the fear of our oppressors

Black culture was removed from our lives

Let's begin with the history of mammy

Which lasted through the era of Jim Crow

This is what they called Black women

Wherever they would go

They called us pickaninnies and mammies

And displayed us on postcards, kitchenware, and toys

Black women couldn't get no respect

Not even from little girls and boys

But Black hair was such a wonder

That many wished they could deny

A Black woman could grow hair so big

That not even the laws of gravity could defy

Freed Black women would embellish their hair with jewels

Their hair styles were alluring and fly

And many white men began to take notice

Whenever they saw a Black queen pass them by

So, in the 1820s, the governor of Louisiana

Required Creole women to cover their hair

Because Black hair was so enticing

And biracial children were coming from everywhere

Today some Sistah's may not know their history

It seems like headwraps have lost their place

That's why we must recall our heritage

'Cause headwrap shouldn't be seen as a disgrace

Remember how we made it look regal

To wear those majestic headwraps

We used them as a symbol of resistance

Sistah's was like, "we're taking our power back"

Because headwraps are more than fashion

In Africa, they represent one's status in life

Whether you're a grieving widow

A revered grandmother

Or a man's beloved wife

That's one reason why history is important

It helped our ancestors find their way

To combat those negative images

From a time when they once were slaves

Now you know the history of the headwrap

And how it has been preserved through hurt and shame

So, we must never forget that it was out of Africa

That the majestic head piece came

Peace and Blessing to the American Sistah's

Who represent the red, black, and green

It's up to you to teach the truth about

The headwrap's purpose and what it really means

Because we are the mothers of nations

And your natural beauty is more than enough

So, be proud and bold about Black culture

'Cause you are representing a part of us

This is how we honor our ancestors

In a respectful and beautiful way

'Cause it's up to us to preserve our history

No matter what other folks may say

So, tell them that

This is not just some rag

That we wear upon our heads

This is a majestic intertwining

Of vibrant colors and woven threads

This headwrap is a signal

That lets them other folks know

That the Black woman will always be a queen

Wherever she may go!

APHRODESIAC

Listen, Bro!

I know I'm beautiful and Black

You could say that I'm something

Like an aphrodesiac!

I know my afro puffs

Got major impact

Hard to believe I'm thirty-five

And I still ain't cracked

You seem confident and fine

And that's a sho nuff fact

But my melanin's got you so shook

That you don't know how to act!

They say game recognize game

So, I kicked it right back

Yeah, the chemistry was alright

But your game is kinda whack!

I know "you can't be in love that fast

Bruh, you really need to relax

Take a chill and keep your feelings in tack

Before you end up getting sidetracked"

I can tell you feeling me

You diggin' the way my curves are stacked

But I think maybe it's my pheromones

That got you under attack

So, please slow your roll

Or your soul might get jacked

By this beautiful and black

aphrodesiac!

BIG, BLACK, & BEAUTIFUL

Put your crown on Sis

Don't believe that old myth

'Cause Brotha's don't think you're fat

They say you're "beautiful and thick"!

And I know a lot of men out here

That love to see you work those hips

So, let those haters keep talking

'Cause some men see your weight as a gift

Listen, I ain't throwing no shade

'Cause being slim is also great

But some Brotha's like a woman

Who can put some extra meat on his plate

Big and beautiful

Can also be a preferred taste

For men who like women

Who are pretty in the face

And thick in the waist

You don't need to be derailed

By those numbers on the scale

'Cause beauty goes deeper than your skin

No matter if you are thick or thin

But the most important thing

Is that you stay healthy and fit

And, I promise, those men will be begging

To taste your lips

Gurl, ain't nobody perfect

Believe me, you are worth it

One day, you'll find true love

'Cause, Girlfriend, you deserve it

Listen, keep on doing you

And your natural glow will shine through

And continue to carry yourself

Like a queen is supposed to

Now, rock that crown Sis

And stop believing in that old myth

'Cause Brotha's don't think you're fat

They think you're "beautiful and thick"!

I WAS BORN A QUEEN

Being a queen

Doesn't mean I won't fall or slip

But what you ain't gone see

Is me caught up in other people's shit

No matter how many bricks

I've had thrown at me

I'm still rising to the top

'Cause I'm that type of queen!

But I've learned that sometimes

I have to let some people go

Sometimes it's my own blood

That don't wanna see me grow

And some folks only come around

To put on a good show

Yeah, they think they know me

But they really don't know

Of course, it's sad

That I've had to struggle and fight

But that's because our people are so divided

That it's almost impossible for us to unite

But what I'm not gone do

Is to be out here looking

Like "Boo-boo the Fool"

'Cause I'm from the old school

I can tell a hard rock from a jewel

I'm about love and peace

Because I move like a queen

But if I you try to come for me

I'll get a jar of Vaseline

Baby, I'm a grown-ass woman

And I stay in my own lane

I've healed from my traumas

I'm too old for the b.s. and the games

But if ya'll start some mess with me

You can go and call the police

After I finish dragging your behind

All up and down these streets

'Cause some of y'all be living

Like *The Young and the Restless*

And I work way too hard

To be caught up in something senseless

So, please don't try me

Or "you gon' learn today"

And I really don't have the time

'Cause I got bills to pay

I'm a queen, not Burger King

No, you cannot have it your way

Keep acting like crabs in a bucket

And there will' be some hell to pay

Why do folks create so much karma

And block their own blessings

Ya'll should be focused on getting your bag

'Cause it's the coins you should be collecting

Seems like every day

There's a new street episode

Somebody starts running their mouth

And then they end up cold

Seems like ya'll playing in the dark

Instead of looking for the guiding light

We too busy arguing with each other

But that ain't the enemy we need to fight

Like I said, I'm a real one, Son

I'm both woke and pro-Black

I'm a real one, Fam

So, you really need to fall back

Yeah, I'm a strong Black woman

That's how I was raised!

My mamma taught me well

Believe me, game recognize game

Like I said, being a true queen

Doesn't mean I won't fall or slip

But what you ain't gone see

Is me caught up in other people's shit

No matter how many bricks

I've had thrown at me

I'm keep on rising to the top

'Cause I was born a queen!

I SEE YOU, SIS

Sis, I see you holding it down

Even when you feel broken inside

Yet, no matter how many obstacles you encounter

Just like the sun, you continue to rise!

Remember that strength doesn't come from outer beauty

Your worth and value is not determined by your size

And it sure ain't about wearing lashes so heavy

That people can barely see your eyes

Yeah, I know you got this, Sis!

No matter what others may say or do

And I was really sorry to hear that

Your man was out there cheating on you

I'm glad you changed your number

'Cause now that loser is permanently deleted

And I'm sorry about your disloyal friends

Who weren't there for you

When you needed

Sis, I know some days you feel lonely

Sometimes you wonder if anyone cares

Just know that I'm always keeping you and yours

In my thoughts and prayers

So, keep ya head up, Queen

And take some time to heal

You're probably gonna need a moment

To recover from such a painful ordeal

'Cause life is a marathon

And this is not how it ends

Believe me, can't nobody dim your light

When you glow from within

Sometimes you gotta trust the process

There are lessons we all must learn

And, sometimes, the bigger your heart

The more you end up getting burned

Sis, I see you!

Working hard at two jobs to survive

Buying unhealthy foods

To keep your family alive!

Even when your job underpays you

You gracefully take it in stride

It's okay to ask for some help

With the cost of food prices being so high

I remember when you lost your job

And how you took it all in stride

You got in your feelings for a minute

'Cause it was a little hard on your pride

But then you found a better job

And it became easier to provide

You even took some online classes

To keep your dreams alive

So, never allow life to make you bitter

Don't get caught up in defeat

Just wipe that dust off your behind

And get back up on your feet

Don't just listen to what other folks say

Watch what they do

No matter how many missteps you make

They can't stop the tenacity inside of you

Sometimes you have to walk alone

When you've had more than your share of pain

That's why you ain't got time for no clowns

Tell them you're not looking to be entertained

It's natural to crave affection

Believe me, Sis, I get it

But if people can't add to your peace

Then walk away, don't even sweat it

Some will take your kindness for weakness

And wanna play you like some kind of fool

So, be mindful when it comes to your heart

And be more selective about the partner you choose

I know it's hard but don't let your kids

See you angry or bitter

Remember to keep your eye on the prize

'Cause you weren't raised to be no quitter!

Because the children are our future

And you must never forget that fact

Keep doing what you gotta do

Even if some folks don't have your back

Sis, keep on doing you

Take time to heal if you feel broken inside

I know that despite the obstacles you encounter

Just like the sun, you will continue to rise!

WE WEAR CROWNS, BOO

I've seen some dirty shit

And I've done some slick shit, too

I've got a lot of friends

But I got a lot of haters, too

If you see a Brooklyn Queen walk by

Here's what you should do

Show her much respect

'Cause we wear crowns over here, Boo!

I used to play those mind games

I've seen a lot of that in the hood

I keep a hustle on the side

To make sure that my family eats' good!

When it comes to a Brooklyn queen

We ain't nothing like the rest

We let you know from the jump

We won't settle for nothing less

Brooklyn Queens like to flex

We always try to look our best

Some of us are spiritual

That's why we got the ankh around our neck

You can see the swag in the walk

You can hear Brooklyn when we talk

We work hard every day

So, we can pull up like a Boss

So, if you ever come to Brooklyn

You need to learn the streets well

'Cause if you ain't from the block

Me and my people can definitely tell

We don't mind, if you wanna shoot your shot

But Bruh, please don't take all day

'Cause Brooklyn queen's keep it moving

Listen, we got bills to pay

Body smells like coconut and mango butter

And the melanin is always on fleek

Sometimes we'll smile back

Sometimes we won't even speak

Seems like whatever we eat

It goes straight to our hips

I guess we're naturally thick

Or maybe, it's the fish and grits

Queens are more than a snack

We'll leave you satisfied like a feast

We keep things on the down low

But we'll turn you out in the sheets

We don't care for a slice

We want the whole dang pie

And if you tryna go Dutch?

Keep ya money, Little Boy! Goodbye!

So yeah, I've seen some dirty shit

And I've done some slick shit, too

I got a lot of friends

But I got a lot of haters too

If you see a Brooklyn Queen walk by

Here's what you should do

Show her much respect

'Cause we wear crowns over here, Boo!

CAUGHT UP IN THE SYSTEM

Brotha, you had me when you smiled and said,

"Power to the people, my sister!"

You stood there looking powerful and bold

While I felt weak like an aimless drifter

You offered me the red pill like "Morpheus"

You helped my chakras align

You taught me about spirituality

And then you opened my mind

Brotha you already had me!

You were willing to give me your time

You enlightened me on a higher level

I was no longer dumb, deaf, or blind

It seems like you caught me

Right in the nick of time

I was sinking into a deep depression

I felt like I was ready to resign

But you saw my hunger for truth

You treated me with respect

You helped me discover my purpose

Your wisdom had a profound effect!

You taught me to ask the right questions

And that all actions should be measured

You helped me find my path

Knowing you has truly been a pleasure

Now, I can see the traps in the system

I've removed the seeds of indoctrination

Now I know that Black folks have been set up

For the worse possible situations

I'm sure it's not a coincidence

That we're given poorest education

That's why Black families have to do better

When it comes to teaching the next generation

Thank you for schooling me on why

Society wants to see us divided and weak

Why the privileged say poor folks are the problem

Yet they allow drugs and weapons on our streets

They'd rather see us fighting each other

Instead of coming together for peace

They fear Blacks and Whites uniting

To use the power of freedom of speech

You explained the post traumatic trauma

And how we have been mentally conditioned

And that when Black folks ask for help

No one really wants to listen

And how they twist and bend the laws

For the powerful and the rich

But they tell us justice is blind

Like we're supposed to fall for that shit ?

Instead, they engage in destructive wars

Between Muslims, Christians and Jews

They bomb innocent men, women and children

While we watch them die with no medication or food

Big corporations don't want to lower prices

Our people are crying for assistance

The homeless population increases

And folks become diabetic from poor nutrition

Yet the system is protecting the wealthy

While treating the poor with disdain and hostility

Some want to defund social programs

And reduce aid for seniors and those with disabilities

Now I know why freedom isn't free

And why America was built off the backs of Black people

How they use to trade Black bodies for money on wall street

'Cause the constitution never really saw us as equals

Yet, we continue fighting to break the chains

Of racism, prejudices and discrimination

Now I will never allow them to treat me

Like I'm not a part of this nation

White supremist fear their slow decline

Soon the minorities will be the majority

I believe that one day we'll all be free

When righteous leaders begin to govern with authority

But, I still remember the day when you smiled

And said ,"Power to the people, my sister!"

You stood there looking powerful and bold

While I felt as weak as an aimless drifter

You gave me the red pill

You helped my chakras align

You taught me about spirituality

Thank you so much, for opening my mind!

THE QUEEN PROTECTS THE KING

Listen, if you've got me

Then I've got you, King!

As long as you have my back

You ain't gotta worry about a thing

We can be a power couple

A strategic mind is what I bring

But I'm talking about a bond for life

Not some frivolous fling

I'll always stand with you

And my word is my bond

There's nothing for you to fear

Because an allegiance has been formed

It's the queen who protects the king

And believe me, my game is strong!

'Cause when you have a queen by your side

You can never be played like a pawn

So, let me offer you my counsel

For all that glitters isn't gold

Some women may be more attractive

But they can have a rotten soul

So, keep your eyes on the goal

Even a friend can commit treason

Don't let your guard down so quick

Don't become too appeasing

It's better to choose quality

And let your inner circle decrease

Having a lot of friends is fine

But nothing's more valuable than your peace

Some don't wanna see you winning

But I'll always encourage you to grow

Some just wanna take your spot

But a queen will always let you know

And I promise to protect your crown

'Cause life can be like a game of chess

I'm speaking from the heart

Better watch your next step

Sometimes a king can fall short

And some don't see the intercept

Cause' we all have lessons in life

That we still haven't mastered yet

Remember to stand in your truth

Never live life with regrets

Don't let a woman's beauty leave you blind

That low-level thinking is incorrect

Don't be controlled by your desires

Let your queen relieve that stress

And when you need to recharge

That means it's time for you to rest

You gotta give a queen your loyalty

If you want her respect

Then watch your kingdom grow

And become the man that you profess

As long as we remain united

Her heart can never be questioned

As long as you remain true

She'll give you all of her affection

Yeah, this life of chess

Can truly be a challenge

But your home and your heart

Should always be in balance

Just stay ahead of the game

And never be too complacent

Our dreams will come true

But we have to be patient

And when the enemy comes for us

We remain calm,

We don't overreact

This game is ours to win

We'll be prepared to fight back!

So, if you got me

Then I got you, King!

As long as you have my back

You ain't gotta worry about a thing

Together we're a power couple

A strategic mind is what I bring

I'm talking about a bond for life

Not some frivolous fling

I'll always stand with you

And my word is my bond

There's nothing for you to fear

Because an allegiance has been formed

Remember, the queen protects the king

And my game is strong!

And as long as you have me by your side

You'll never be played like a pawn!

GODDESS WITHIN

She is Mother Earth,

Who has the power of birth.

She is Goddess of the Moon.

She is Goddess Oshun.

She is Goddess Nut,

Who controls the sky.

She has the power to swallow the sunset,

And give birth to the sunrise.

She is Goddess Ma'at. Oh, can't you see.

She is the keeper of balance and harmony.

She is the protector from evil and foes.

She is Goddess Wadjet whom everyone knows.

She is the goddess who uses the Eye Of Heru.

This is the source where true power comes through.

She is goddess of pleasure and goddess of the sacred cat.

She the beautiful goddess known as Bastet.

Standing in your power,

A lioness is born.

Queen of the Nile River,

Slender and long.

All of the elements shall move at a goddess's command,

For she is the wind that blows the sand.

So, Queen, when you discover your goddess within,

Fear not, Beloved, for your journey is about to begin.

THE OPEN MIC BLUES

IF I WERE A POEM

If…if…if…

I…I…I…

Were…were…were…

A…a…a…

Poem…poem…poem…

I'd be so dope

That it would seem ridiculous

I'd be very, very Black, and articulate

Every spoken word would be meticulous

I'd be as fearless as an abolitionist

I'd bless you more than St. Nicholas

I'd do more than just "kick it"

I'd take your mind from rags to riches

Like a winning Powerball ticket

And you'd be blowing up my phone

Like I worked for Cricket

If I were a poem

I'd capture your senses

Like a sweet perfume

I'd give you lyrical rhymes and rhythm

Like Black Music History in June

I'd be hot and smoking

Like a sexy jazz tune

Wearing a black sequin dress

With some red-bottom shoes

If I were a poem

I'd be the missing link

I'd make you all wanna think

I'd break every chain

And take your imaginations to the brink

'Cause if I were a poem

We would all be in sync

If I were a poem

I'd be a literary legacy

Copyrights would be a necessity

I'd give you history notes

With no discrepancies

And my wordplay would feel like weaponry

If I were a poem

I'd be an open book

I'd be easy to read

I'd be like reparations

I'd put your mind at ease

I'd be cleaning spirits like sage

Make it easier to breathe

I'd be burning down trees

With the ancestors' blood

On the leaves

I'd be someone like Nat Turner

Who tried to set the slaves free

And I'd open the gates of Heaven

So, y'all wouldn't need no key

If I were a poem

I'd be someone's salvation

I'd be like a spiritual vacation

I'd unite the populations

And liberate minds from incarceration

If I were a poem

I'd meet you at the crossroads

I'd make your cup overflow

I'd be spitting Negro spiritual codes

And saving Black folks by the boat load

While bumping to Dre's "Next Episode"

If I were a poem

I'd be tapping on your thoughts

Like I was "Mr. Bojangles"

I'd have metaphors bouncing off the floors

From all angles

I'd be like Goddess Oshun

Willfully changing the tides

I'd show you signs so divine

You'll think you've lost your mind

If I were a poem

I'd fix this capitalist world order

And show you how to live in a world

With no wars and no borders

I'd rip off the Band-Aid

And awaken the sleepwalkers

I'd write an ode to the ancestors

Who transitioned in the Atlantic waters

If I were a poem

I'd break every generational curse

If you still felt neglected

Then I would give you love first

If you needed libation

Then I'd quench your thirst

If you had a broken spirit

Then I'd become your nurse

And if you feared for your life

I'd tell you about the rebirth

Because

If…if…if…

I…I…I…

Were…were…were…

A…a…a…

Poem…poem…poem…

I'd be the most prolific poem on earth!

MR. POETRY

Yeah, I fell in love with a guy

Named Mr. Poetry

And my life ain't been the same

Since he stepped to me

He's got a cool ass vibe

Cool as an autumn breeze

He said,

"Why don't you let me put you on top

Where you're supposed to be?"

He said I had great possibility

But that I was missing the key

So, he took me under his wing

And set my poetry flag free

You see,

We didn't just cross paths

On some two-way street

'Cause he and I

Were destined to meet

And I know why he likes me!

'Cause I'm so feisty

He gives me food for thought

And that excites me

His metaphors entice me

His stanzas delight me

Mr. Poetry makes me

Wanna do it like Nike

But for real though

We take it real slow

He ain't the

Average Joe

He helps me heal, yo

I mean right off the bat

His main focus was me

He showed me true love

And he did it openly

He poured into my cup

And put some hope in me

'Cause there was something about

The way he spoke to me

He loved me patiently

Said he would wait for me

Told me he had faith in me

And built a place for me

Never played tricks

Or tried to elude me

He pierced my thoughts

And he vigorously pursued me

Now we communicate

With poetic exchanges

And he arouses my intellect

With factual phrases

And that's the reason why

I sing his praises

'Cause he makes me spill my ink

All over his pages

I remember when he first

Entered my imagination

He took me from average

To having higher expectations

Now we use wordplay to converse

That's our source of communication

And we use critical thinking

To a have deeper conversation

But sometimes we go

Blow for blow

And stand toe-to-toe

Yeah, we be slamming

But we keep that on the low

And when it's late at night

We binge on metaphors like food

'Cause I be drawn to his page

Like Billie was drawn to the Blues

Yeah, I'm so sprung on his verses

I wanna spread the news

I wanna count all his syllables

'Cause he gives me Haikus

And now my pen

Has a stronger foundation

Now, I'm a professional writer

Who's paid to give demonstrations

So yeah, I'm in love with a guy

Named Mr. Poetry

And my life ain't been the same

Since he stepped to me

Yeah, he's got a cool ass vibe

Cool as an autumn breeze

And now I'm sitting on top

Right where I'm supposed to be

I'LL TELL YOU NO LIE

Let me tell you this

And I tell you no lie

The revolution

The revolution

The revolution will not be televised

And it won't be

Advertised

Commercialized

Disenfranchised

Or Capitalized

Let me say this one mo' time

And no, I'm not high

Just look at my eyes

Okay, I see you have some questions

So, allow me to clarify

It won't come from your

Worst enemy

Nor will it come from your

Very best friend

And it definitely will not be seen on

CBS

NBC

Or

CNN

The revolution ain't concerned about

Your church denomination

Your political party affiliations

Or any religious confrontations

And it don't care

If you ain't got a dime to your name

Or whether you own a lot of stocks

And it sure don't care about no

Fat man who slid down a chimney

Just to leave you a gift box

It won't be found on IG

Or in some social media post

It won't be found on BET

And it won't be found in Oprah's

Key to life and happiness quotes

The revolution

Will not be bothered

With your new job

Your new social status

Or your latest obsession

It won't care about your privileges

Or your desires

Or whose gone win the next election

No, it's not about that treasonous

Capitol Hill insurrection

Nor does it care about

Your small-minded beliefs

Or your opinionated objections

Now pay close attention and listen

'Cause this announcement

Will not be broadcasted

Or underwritten

I said, "The revolution will not be televised"

No, I ain't bullshittin'!

'Cause it won't be found on

Your tablet

Your watch

Or your new iPhone

And it doesn't care if you're real popular

Or if you walk alone

Oh, and please believe that

The revolution will not be overseas

Nor will it be in some luxury vacation home

That's being observed by some secret drone

It won't care

If you're a vegetarian

A "fruitarian"

Or a carnivore who eats meat

Because the real question is

"Have you found your peace?"

Listen, ladies and gentlemen

The revolution is about

More than being

Pro-masculine or

Pro-feminine

And, of course, it can always

Use some more melanin

It don't care about

How many sexual partners you've had

That was your decision

But it cares about a woman's right to choose

Without asking a man for his permission

The revolution isn't about passing judgment

Because it doesn't give a blip

It doesn't care about the size of your ego

Or about where you might have slipped

'Cause the revolution is coming

And ya'll better believe that shit!

The revolution is not concerned with

Who's losing and who's winning

Just as long as the earth

Keeps on revolving and spinning!

It's about a different operation

And a different situation

And making sure that your souls survives

During this transformation!

It's not about who's to blame

Or who has the most responsibility

It's about living in a world filled with chaos

While remaining in a state of tranquility!

It's not about trying to fit in

Or going against the norm

It's about how you're gonna come out

On the other side of the storm!

So, let me tell you this

And I'll tell you no lie

The revolution

The revolution

The revolution will not be televised!

I ONLY DATE SAPIOSEXUALS

(A sapiosexual is a person who is attracted to intelligence)

Listen, I don't care what nobody say,

I only date sapiosexuals

Because sapiosexuals

Are highly intellectual

And they really know how to vibe

With a conscious Afrosexual

Because the level of the conversation

Can be so impeccable

That every word seems

Down-

-Right

Delectable!

But I know how to keep it professional

I mean, nice and respectable

But believe me, there's nothing

More exceptional

Than a thought-provoking sapiosexual!

But sometimes sapios can be

More friendly than sexual

They wanna get to know you first

Before things really get technical

So, no matter if the attraction is detectable

And the arousal is unquestionable

The contemplations of a sapiosexual

Can be extremely flexible!

But non-intellectuals just wanna see

If a woman is thick or slender

And decide which way to bend her

They just wanna get her

nice and tender

And make her surrender

Then turn around and act

Like they don't remember

They seem to be more like

Lustful pretenders

Just looking for

Easy vendors

And promiscuous lenders

With freaky fetishes

And hidden agendas

Most of them just wanna

Lay next to you

And get wet with you

So, they can have sex with you

And when they're done

They'll send a goodbye text to you

'Cause they really didn't have

Much respect for you!

And their mood swings

Can become so erratic

They prowl around like

Sexual nympho addicts

And seductive nomadics

Who are indecisive

But wanna hit it like rabbits!

Because they have the most

Self-destructive habits

That can become so problematic

And cause a lot of havoc

Which is why they usually come

With a whole lot of baggage

But I'll never be that stressed

'Cause I don't deal with that mess!

I don't waste my time on foolishness

And I'm very direct

I speak my mind well

And I like to get things off my chest

That's why I only date sapios

Because they know how to come correct

So yes, I've got

Love and respect

For those sexy intellects

They've got so much swag

When they rock the latest specs

They hang out at bookstores

More than the gym

'Cause knowledge is the real flex

They keep the convo 100

Nerds don't need to be complex

Sometimes you might see them

Pull up to Barnes & Noble

In the BMW or the Lex!

Listen, my type is

Geeky but still freaky

The type to keep them

Credit scores squeaky!

I like the sexy professors

Who give private lectures

I like the sexy dudes

With the high IQs

Sometimes I'll let him come through

So, he can teach me something new

Sip a lil' wine and play a game of Taboo

Yeah, we be drinking and thinking

And letting that knowledge sink in

And then we'll play a little Scrabble

Until my legs unravel

That's why I have a personal preference

And I do my own assessment

We'll talk about investments

And snack on some refreshments

And if the convo was good

I might give him a reference

So, if you wanna date a sapiosexual

Here's my suggestion

Stop beating around the bush

But make a good impression

Okay

Time's up!

And this concludes our session

Unless you have some more

Relevant questions

About today's lesson

So, you see

This is why I only date sapiosexuals

Because sapiosexuals

Are highly intellectual

And they really know how to vibe

With a conscious Afrosexual

Because the level of the conversation

Can be so impeccable

That every word seems

Down-

-Right

Delectable!

But I always keep it professional

You know, nice and respectable

Believe me, there's nothing

More exceptional

Than a thought-provoking sapiosexual!

GODDESS ON THE MIC

I'm proud to be a poet

And I have a talent for blessing the mic

I guess you can say that I'm gifted

Cause' I'm really that nice!

Folks say I'm a "Fannie Lou Hamer

Meets Maya Angelou" type

'Cause when I speak my truth

I sound like a goddess on the mic!

Some say I sound like a rhyme master

When I start to recite

But no matter what I write

I always bring truth to the light

And sometimes I just might

Go to a poetry spot at night

'Cause I know that's the place

Where great minds think alike

Yes, I may be different

But let me make this perfectly clear

I only wanna give you the gospel truth

And my words are definitely sincere

Hey, you don't have to take my word for it

Just watch and listen

And see my ancestors' wildest dreams

Come to fruition

Now, don't shoot the messenger

Cause' I want you to hear this message

Learn to read between the lines

That's where you'll find the blessings

And don't fall for them fake prophets

Who just wanna dig in your pockets

It's a shame how some folks

Are only looking to make a profit

They say they're trying to save you

By telling you certain Scriptures

They preach a whole sermon

But they never give you the whole picture

And some just wanna take advantage

Of those in poor circumstances

Like the ones looking for forgiveness

And second chances

But I came here to be a blessing

To the old and the new

Consider this my new testament

Allow me to expand your point of view

Listen, I'm a firm believer

That knowledge is in the hands of the reader

And righteous wisdom is conceived

In the mind of the perceiver

And we'll never elevate minds

If we're arguing and fighting all the time

Seems like division and confusion

Are signs of the time

But here's some food for thought

Keep your vibrations high

Focus on reaching your higher self

Instead of paying those tithes

'Cause the truth is that God

Is already inside of you

Listen, you don't have to be a saint

To get a seat in my pew

Yes I've got a beef with the greedy

Because they prey on the needy

So, whoever got a problem with that

You can tell them to come and see me!

I've heard that practice makes perfect

I've been tested, now I'm ready

'Cause iron sharpens iron

And I'm sharp as a machete

I just happen to be lyrically gifted

And spiritually appointed

My pen has been exalted

And I'm poetically anointed

Now I may speak like a goddess

But here's what you need to understand

Just ' because I'm spiritual

Don't mean you can't catch these hands!

Truthfully, I've gotta love jones

For blessing the microphone

And I'll be hitting it like a former slave

Who's coming for everything

They said I couldn't own

And that's the power that I hold

As a Black creative

It's the spirit of my ancestors

That makes me sound so persuasive

Now, I hope you don't let this

Pretty face fool you!

'Cause my third eye stays open

And I can see right through you!

I know that words have the power

To break generational curses

That's why I put a whole lot of thought

Into writing my poetic verses

So, when I step to the mic

I'm bringing all the smoke

'Cause a lot of y'all are still sleeping

But I wanna see you woke!

And I wish they would come for me

So, I can put their thoughts in a yoke

Look, I said what I said

I ain't playing with those folks

Listen, poets are the real story tellers

That's why I'm a proud MVP

Believe me, every verse that I spit

Is meant to set y'all free

But I hope it's clear by now

That when you're looking at me

It's more like a thousands of my ancestors

That you really see!

That's why I'm proud to be a poet

And I have a talent for blessing the mic

I guess you can say that I'm gifted

Cause' I'm really that nice!

Folks say I'm a "Fannie Lou Hamer

Meets Maya Angelou" type

'Cause when I speak my truth

I sound like a goddess on the mic!

A RUDE AWAKENING

Some folks love to sing our Blues

But don't know the history of being Black

So, as your local neighborhood poet

It's my job to give you some of the facts

Being Black means telling our history

Feels like food for the soul

I know that some folks might not get it

But telling our truth never gets old

Being Black feels like the Blues

Sometimes it's served with an Afrobeat

With the power of the Djembe

That makes you wanna move your feet

Being Black means that we carry our pain

Like generational curses on our backs

But it also means that when we get knocked down

We know how to stand up and hit back

Being Black means we gotta work twice as hard

But our contributions are not easily recognized

This may come as a rude awakening but,

Black inventions have benefited all American lives

Being Black means being extraordinarily creative

We've even made houses out of chicken bones

It was the enslaved Africans who brought the skills

To build the white house that our presidents call home

Black folks are the maestros of music

We are the King and Queens of Soul

And when it comes to American music

It's the melanated folks that are in control!

Being Black means being the trendsetters

It means being our ancestors' wildest dreams

It means Black folks speak with Black codes

So, what you hear, ain't always what it means

Being Black means we have Black people time

Which is why Black folk have a habit of being late

Being Black don't mean we have to be best friends

For us to check and see if you're straight

Of course, if a Black person sees you running

They don't ask no questions; they just get up and run

But it's peculiar how Black folks end up in a chokehold

While Non-Blacks are the shooters with automatic guns

Now, I don't know if you've heard

About the American "one-drop rule"

It says that if you have just one drop of

Black blood running through your veins

That means you're Black, too

Yeah, some folks love to sing our Blues

But don't know the history of being Black

So, as your local neighborhood poet

It has been my pleasure to give you some of the facts

A TREE WITHOUT ROOTS

It's 2024 and we're still failing
Because we are like shallow trees without roots
We've forgotten the lessons of our past
And we believe the lies, with no shred of proof!

We've stopped helping each other
And we've stopped teaching our youth
But our people cannot grow and thrive
As long as we are starving for the truth

Still wrestling with our identities
As generations grow up misbelieving
Look at how our seeds are struggling
I say "it's time for a new season"

Should we make our way to the motherland?
We've got more than enough reasons
Let's create a Black utopia
That we can all believe in

They will never give up their power
And the odds will never be even
But if we can build and work together

Then we won't actually need them!

Remember how they destroyed our Black families
Then they forced us into poor neighborhoods
They casually kill our unarmed brothers and sisters
And then they say that Black folks are "no good" ?

They plotted to give us welfare
And they denied us good paying jobs
They told us about the American Dream
While we were steadily being robbed

Now many can't afford decent housing
Because of neighborhood gentrification
They have money to pay for wars
Yet they can't find a dime for reparations

We are the ones who made it possible
For them to build the United States
There would be no American country
If it wasn't for the help of the Black race

They know that we are still struggling
Because living expenses are too great
Maybe if we would pool Black resources

Poor families could live in a better place

Tell me who's looking out for Black families
It's getting harder and harder to make ends meet
When Black folks make it out of the ghetto
Some turn their back on the streets

How can we tear each other down
After our ancestors paid such a heavy price
Remember that Dr. King died
So that we could live a better life

Why have Black women become so hypersexual
Walking around half-naked and showing their ass
Sistas, how can you teach your seeds
If you're out here selling yourselves for cash?

Young lady stop letting these little boys
Call y'all tricks and hoes
And Black man
You're not my "nigga"
Brother you are my "bro"!

Sistas, our men show us no respect
While the world sits back and laugh

Remember that you are mothers of nations
Don't allow them to dishonor your past

Do you recall how they destroyed Black Wall Street
Because they knew we were too powerful together
They were jealous of our Black businesses
They didn't want us to invest in our own endeavors

So, let's come together and rebuild
Let's create Black businesses in every city
Our people deserve much more than
The government's unsympathetic pity

It's 2024 and we're still failing to thrive
Because we are like shallow trees without roots
We've forgotten the lessons of our past
And we believe their lies, with no shred of proof!

We've stopped helping each other
And we've stopped teaching our youth
But our people will not grow and thrive
As long as we are starving for the truth

POETIC BOMBSHELLS

Now, listen here, Cuz

I'm gon' make it do what it does

But first I gotta say

I'm not the person I once was

'Cause when I broke out of my shell

And started casting word spells

I learned to make Black books sell

By dropping my poetic bombshells

I remember when I was a young Black girl

Who wanted to learn about Black history

When I found that it was missing from my textbooks

I had a real epiphany!

'Cause it seemed that my heritage

Was some kind of mystery

So, I learned more about our culture

And I memorized every word

I was a little queen who stood in the cipher

And they could not believe what they heard

Yeah, I was a Black girl from the block

Who could spit barz to a beatbox

They said my lyrics were so heavy

They left mental aftershocks

Yeah, I was a proud New Yorker

And I was my mother's daughter

I had a mouth flooded with verses

They said this child can't even hold water

So, I broke out of that a mental prison

I grew tired of that kind of livin'

Like the great Shirley Chilsom

I rejected the nonsense that was given

I was tired of being manipulated

So, I grew to be wise

I started spitten' so many poems

It sounded like bullets in a drive-by

I started learning about strange fruits

And looking out for the youth

Digging into my African roots

So, I could speak on the hidden truth

But on my word

I swear

I'm too original

To be compared

'Cause I got that savoir-faire

And sometimes I speak a little

Shakespeare here and there

And my dialects is so severe

My intellect might fall on deaf ears

But iron sharpens iron

I hope I made that abundantly clear

So, I never have to bite

When I sit down to write

'Cause a real poet knows how

To turn darkness into light

Sometimes I'll spit something new

When I get an inclination

Just like I can whip up a sauce

For my next creation

Some say I write like

A poetic genius

Cause I can rise from the ashes

Of a burning phoenix

So, like I said, Cuz

I'm gon' make it do what it does

But I had to let you know

I'm not the person I once was

'Cause when I broke out of my shell

And started casting word spells

I learned to make Black books sell

By dropping my poetic bombshells

SOUL-SNATCHING BLUES

HIS WORDS

His words played me like a melody

As the liquor from his tongue

Washed over me like rainwater

Cleansing my muddy soul

Bringing out the jazz from my Blues

And causing me to give birth to a brand new tune

I felt his words arousing my intellect

Like the sun rising in my soul

He was giving me life

His words surpassed my threshold

I can't explain why he's got such a hold on me

Each word penetrating my emotions

He became the air I wanted to breathe

He showed me a new sense of stimulation

I became inebriated by his verbal conversations

He took away my pain like spiritual medication

I fell in love with his brand of gin

And oh, how I fantasized about tasting him

Thinking his skin might be even sweeter than his words

And that somehow his flesh would satisfy my craving

'Cause I was more than ready

For some misbehaving

So, I kicked back, and I listened

I listened while his elixir

Slowly dripped from his tongue

To his poetic lips

The syllables from his dialect

Provoked a sway in my hips

Oh, how I swooned to the music in his words

Every syllable played on my heart strings

I felt him arouse my deepest emotions

The way he filled me with his energy was everything

Until once again I sat there

Patiently waiting to be served

Another deep dish

Of his magnificent words

SENSUAL SYMPHONY

This maestro was so skillful

He was making her lose her way

Spinning her around

Like an after dark album

That needed to be played

Slowly melting her melancholy away

It was like a sensual symphony!

They had perfect harmony

I mean he was hitting all the right notes

Giving her an out of body experience

That caused her soul to float

Made her wanna praise his name

Releasing the chords in the back of her throat

No need to call the cops

Because this collaboration was dope!

Looks like it's gonna be a sensual symphony!

She was drawn to him like a moth to a flame

And he became her naughty habit

That maestro played her like a harp

With the touch of a masterful pianist

So, she followed his lead

Becoming intoxicated by his wine

'Cause music like this only comes

Once in a lifetime

Even in the dark

Their flames had a powerful glow

He called her a masterpiece

That made him want to flex his toes

Honey child, it was a sensual symphony

Their magic was coursing through the air

Cause this kind of chemistry takes time

The vibe was like southern comfort

Mixed with strawberry wine

He was giving her all that "Mo' Better"

Like a groovy kind of pleasure

It was raining like Lena Hornes' "Stormy Weather"

And Al Green's "Let's Stay together"

Now that's what I call a sensual symphony

They were flowing like a jazz tune

Flowing like some throwback

Soulful Rhythm and Blues

That she would often play

Whenever she had a hard day

He was definitely the conductor

Of her song

He had her humming some of

Marvin Gayes' "What's going on?"

Because this maestro was so skillful

He made her lose her way

And spined her around

Like an after dark album

That needed to be played

Slowly melted her melancholy away

Yeah, I think I need a smoke,

Cause that was a sensual symphony!

FORGET ME NOT

I gave him good loving

Hot biscuits with gravy fresh from my oven

But that wasn't enough

'Cause loving a man like him was rough!

I really thought that I could hang

But pain just ain't my thang

And too many tears left me

Slightly insane

He had me losing my grip

He had me trying to remember

Where I'd slipped

But I was just so mesmerized

By that good-ish

Did I mention that he was

Tall, Dark, and Toned

I couldn't believe how he

Broke me down to the bone!

And then he started chilling at my crib

Like it was his home

But I said, "This can't be

All that is meant for me!

Giving my love to a man

Who will never love me!"

Yet I treated him kind

Pretended to be dumb, deaf, and blind

Thinking one day

I'll make him mine

But I wished I would have walked away

When I saw first saw the signs

I should have caught a clue

When he started playing tricks with my mind

Because now I've come to see

That the joke was really on me

'Cause I was too kind and sweet

And I was just his "sometimes" treat

Now I wish we'd never had met

Now I wish we'd never had sex

Now I wish that a man like him

Was easier for me to forget

HE'S GONE NOW

He's gone now

He left darkness in my eyes

He scorched my soul inside

He compelled me to be wise

He spoon fed me goodbyes

He's out of my life now

Memories pierce my soul

His touch left me cold

I remember when he was mine

To have and to hold

He's moved on now

Left me with shattered dreams

And silent screams

He's left me stitching the seams

Of my broken heart

And shedding my lonely tears in the dark

He's in my past now

So, I have decided to live again

I've mourned and buried him

I've pushed through my pain like a crushing wind

But a shadow of me still reaches out for him

He's long gone now

He gave me the sting of pain

His cruelness did not go in vain

For I am no longer the same

Yet I still shed a tear

When I hear his name

MY KIND OF MAN

I want a man who is proud and free

One who knows who he was born to be

One who does not hide from his true reflection

I need a king who has his own sense of direction

A melanin god – the darker the better

I want a love that will last always and forever

I want a man who has no fear of committing

I want a king who will make me enjoy submitting

A man who will shower me with love and devotion

One who is man enough to show his true emotions

His essence will be strong

And he'll be wearing my favorite scent

I'll worship at his, temple

And my knees will be bent

He'll be at home cooking

When I get there

Meet me at the door

And gently run his fingers through my hair

He will kiss me on my forehead

And ask me about my day

He'll say, "Tell me where it hurts

And I'll make it okay"

He will take me to my limit

Entice me with pleasure and pain

Run his fingers through my locs

And make me moan his name

The type of man who will release

The goddess in me

He'll become one with my soul

He'll become a part of me

FOR A SEASON

There is a reason

Why I met you

The universe sent

Me here to bless you

We met for a reason

Not for a lifetime

But only for a season

I came to teach you how

To dance in the rain

I came to help you say

Goodbye to the hurt and pain

I came to caress you

Like a summer breeze

I came to give you

What you need

I'm truly honored that I met you

Even if only for a short spell

And when the time comes

I will wish you well

Because it was our destiny

To meet for a reason

Not for a lifetime

But only for a season

THE TREASURE OF YOU

What you are cannot be priced

For you are a one man's paradise

And I'm not running any game

I just wanna feel the drip of your rain

So, if the feeling is mutual

"Say my name! Say my name"

I swear on my life this ain't no lie

And you got me putting in work

Like this is my new grind

If only you could see yourself through my eyes

If only I could understand the magic

That God placed between your thighs

Goddess, I'm hoping that the spark

Of this sincere dialect

Results in a cause and effect

That makes our souls connect

It can be at any time

Or any place

On any part of my face

'Cause I want to lay upon your cloud

I want to shoot star dust inside your moon

Venturing upon the crescent of you

For you are so amazing

And those fools must be crazy

To let such bliss slip

Through their fingertips

A man can't help but

Get caught up in your waves

And each time I come crashing down

The more of you I crave

I want to become one with your essence

And inscribe my initials in your cave

And I hope you never turn me away

Because I wanna love you

Until the end of my days

SEXUAL DEMONS

Ooooh, your sexy body will certainly do

'Cause all I wanna do

Is play with you

And lay with you

And you

And yes, you too

I'll fulfill your desires

I will intoxicate you like liquor

One sip

Then another sip

And there goes that zipper

'Cause you're not just making love to me

When our souls share energies

So, please believe

I'm giving you all of me!

And all of he!

And all of them!

And all of she!

So, if you decide to lay with me

As I maneuver with complete duplicity

You will come to see that

I'll never show you how I really feel

And I'll never say what I really mean

So, it will be impossible for you to decipher

Which lie you should believe

But Darling

Don't take this personal, please

I give this same speech to all of you

When it's time for me to leave

So, do stay calm

And remember to breathe

But give this some thought

And take some time to grieve

Now I suppose you're thinking

That I'm just acting cold

But these days people are so fake

I guess keeping it 100

Seems to be bold

Though I never would've had a chance

If you weren't so casual

And thirsty for someone to hold

Because it was your weakness

That made you so easy to control

But no need to worry

By the time I'm through with you

And you

And yes, you too

There will really be nothing

That you can do

And by that time my soul

Will be tied your soul, too

Maybe next time you'll do better

At thinking things through

Maybe you can try a spiritual cleansing

Or focus on something new

Listen, my dear

This is what we sexual demons do

First, we confuse you

Then we use you

It's really too sad

That nobody ever schooled you!

I MISS U

I miss u

I miss u like sand misses the waves

Like an umbrella misses the rain

Like a pilot misses the plane

Like my tongue misses saying your name

I miss u

I miss you like honey misses the tea

Like the forest misses a tree

Like old heads miss R&B

Like Rick James missed Tina Marie

I miss u

I miss u

Like sailors miss curses

Like doctors miss their nurses

Like grandmothers miss their purses

Like Hip-Hop misses verses

I miss u

I miss u like Cracker Jack missed the prize

Like Mother Goose missed the rhymes

Like a clock missed the time

Like Florida missed James on *Good Times*

I miss u

I miss u like mothers miss their kids

Like Adam gave his rib

Like Martin missed Gina

Like the Blues missed Nina

I miss u

I miss u like WWE missed The Rock

Like Jack missed the Box

Like J-Lo missed hanging on the block

Like Black folks missed Michelle and Barack

I miss u

I miss u

I miss u like the pavement misses shoes

Like a piano misses a tune

Like January misses June

Like ice cream misses the spoon

I miss u

I miss u like the way these tears

Miss tissue

'Cause that's how I feel

Whenever I'm not with u

Okay, maybe I am a little obsessed

Okay, fine!

I'm an absolute mess

But if missing u is a sin

Then I do confess!

And I hope it's okay

If I express myself this way

Because these are some of the things

That I just gotta say!

'Cause missing u

Has become my full-time thing

And I'm missing u

Like a park misses the swings

Like winter misses spring

Like a phone that misses a ring!

I know that sounds like some ridiculous thing

But whenever you're not near

My heart does this thing!

Pardon me if I made this such a big issue

But you see my lips are having a fit

Because they wish they could kiss u!

And I would give anything right now

Just be with u

So, I hope you're reading this letter

Because I really do miss u

DO YOU REMEMBER A TIME?

There was a time when the black family was so tight that if one of us was hurting, we all felt it…

A time when children played in the streets with no fear

A time when you had to be home before the streetlights turned on

A time when we had block parties and danced in the street all night

And we settled our differences with a simple street fight

A time when we played ball in the park until the lights came on after dark

A time when we sat around and told stories, amused by the day's events

A time when we stopped and had real conversations with our friends if we saw them on the bus, on the train, or walking down the street

A time when we always waved at Big Momma sitting in the window

because she watched over all of us

A time when your kids could eat at your neighbor's house for dinner

and their kids were welcomed at yours

A time when we would laugh at the neighborhood drunk who

told us jokes and performed for us after one too many drinks, but

we made sure that they got home safe

There was a time when going out on a date meant that we would

walk outside

until the sun came up

A time we when your date walked you to your doorstep and

didn't expect anything in return except the chance

to see you again

There really was a time

Do you remember?

SLIGHTLY FAMILIAR STRANGERS

Hey, what's that you say?

Have we met before?

Was that you who passed by my outside door?

Maybe we're just slightly familiar strangers

Waiting to meet by chance

If only given the right circumstance

I thought of you in my dreams late one night

But I could not see your face in the shimmering light

I hear doorbell rings and all kinds of things

Bringing us one step closer, or so it seems

I see folks walking by

And cars keep on rolling

Still, I sit by my window

Waiting and hoping

I just saw the mailman leave

And I didn't get a letter

They say, "No news is good news"

But I don't feel no better

If, by chance, we happen to meet again

I'll be sure to ask your name

Guess I'll close the window now

'Cause it's starting to smell like rain

Hey, what's that you say?

Have we met before?

I wonder if that was you who passed by my outside door?

HERE I STAND

There she is

And here I stand

Hoping and waiting to be her man

All I long for is that one of these days

She'll lift her head

And look my way

Nothing would please me more

Than on this is day

She should happen to look my way

Last night, I kneeled and prayed

I'm hoping that she feels my presence today

I can fast with no hunger

Because she is all I crave

She doesn't know it yet

But our spirits are engaged

Although we've only made love in my mind

I've replayed it over and over a thousand times

I've been patiently waiting

For her, my soul has been aching

And my heart's anticipating

All the memories we'll be making

Oh, my beautiful lady

You and I will be

But not until she calls for me

Once she's in my arms

She'll be captivated by my charms

And our love will be unmatched

Untamed and unrestrained

I can't wait till the day comes

When she says my name

I'll show her how to spread her wings and fly

And make her glow like candle from the inside

My sweet darling

How I long for the day

The day that she lifts her head

And looks my way

But until that day

Here I will stand

Hoping and waiting to be her man

BLACK MAN, THEY WILL NEVER LOVE YOU LIKE I LOVE YOU

Black Man,

They don't love you

Like I love you!

They will never love you

The way I love you!

'Cause when you bleed, I bleed

All your desires, I will feed

When you take care of my needs

I will bear your seeds

Our love is deeper than any ocean

And surely wider than any sea

Beloved, you are the sustenance

That grows the tree

Our souls could never flourish

In the confines of a plantation shack

So, we chased our freedom

Beyond the railroad tracks

We never knew when

Our enemies would attack

But I knew that I had you

And we had each other's backs

You see

They can't love you

Like I love you

They can't possibly love you

The way I love you

We have an eternal bond

We have that everlasting love

We were taught to pray

To the great ancestors above

Slavery held our flesh in bondage

But we dreamed about what freedom was

That's why Black folks fought in the Civil War

Because being free, was a necessary cause

We were tired of being tortured and enslaved

For so many years

As we waited for the gun smoke

In the South to clear

But no one was there to help us

With our sorrows and fears

When we washed each other's

Blood, sweat and tears

No, they don't love you

Like I love you

There's no way they can love you

The way I love you!

We don't care that one day

We may have to pay a price

Even if that means giving our lives

Because we're too much in love

To live a slave's life

So, let's rejoice in our freedom

Even if we die tonight!

Because with my very last breath

My heart to you I'll give

Because if we can't have love

Then I don't wanna live

Blackman no one will ever understand

What we've been through

And they will never ever love you

The way I love you!

THE ANCESTRAL BLUES

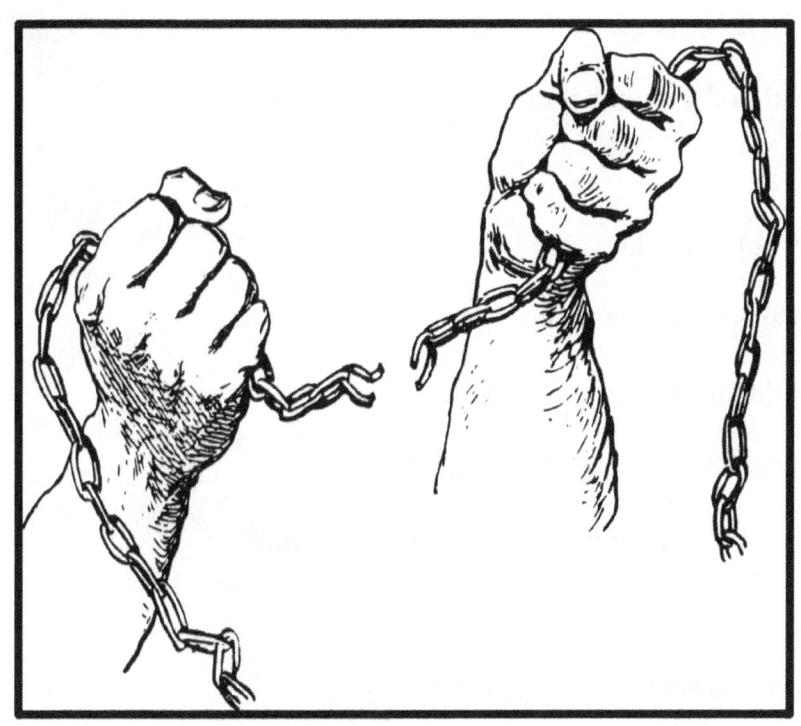

A PLACE CALLED POINT COMFORT

They're taking me to a place called "Point Comfort"

If only I would have known what lay ahead

I would have gotten up earlier to pray

And said everything that needed to be said

I would have kissed my wife tenderly

I would have made sure that my

Children and family had fled

I would have escaped this hideous trauma

And fallen upon my righteous blade instead!

I don't want to go to that place

Called "Point Comfort"

I want my soul to be purged

And I pray to my ancestors

That death comes soon!

I wish to be liberated from this insanity

That I am being forced to consume!

Please set me free from this hell

And let me fly away from this atrocious tomb!

I just couldn't believe my eyes

As I walked through "Point Comfort"

My heart was overwhelmed by grief

When I realized what was planned

There were Black bodies smothered

With palm oil and tar

While those with whips stood in command

Slowly, I made my way

With my shackles scraping through the sand

I saw lustful men waiting at the auction block

Daring to bid on the value of an African man

The stench of their greed filled my nostrils

As they waved money in their sweating hands

But now I fear that when I leave this devil's pit

Called "Point Comfort"

I'll go to a place where brutality is no surprise

I fear there will be no empathy for our suffering

Nor will they bother to wonder

How many of us have died

I sense they won't care about how

They destroyed our sacred bonds

Or disregarded our family ties

And how they eradicated our languages and identities

Just to control every aspect of our lives!

The best any of us can do now

Is to find new ways for our people to survive

Let us create signal songs

And call them "Negro Spirituals"

To secretly help runaways stay alive

There will also come a time when Black people

Will become contrabands of war

And we will fight for equal rights and liberties

And that there will be a place called "Fort Monroe"

Where we will go after years of terror and captivity

I can see a future of reconstruction
And an era of the "KKK" and "Jim Crow"
But this country won't be able to escape
Its perilous past
Where the first seeds of racism were sown

Black people will always be haunted by this place

Called "Point Comfort"

Because if only we would have known what laid ahead

We would have gotten up earlier to pray

And said everything that needed to be said!

We would have kissed our wives tenderly
And made sure that our children and family had fled
Maybe we could have escaped this hideous trauma
And fallen upon our righteous blades instead!

MRS. TUBMAN'S RAILROAD

My name is Araminta Ross

I was born a slave

But I believe that everyone has the right

To freedom or the grave

They say I'm wanted dead or alive

And to that I say, "Please make my day"

Yeah, good luck with all that!

'Cause I'm that one who got away

I was born with a fighting spirit

That made it impossible for me to stay

Because God already told me

That I was unfit to be any man's slave

What they did to Black folks

Was immoral and improper

But like the Scripture says

"No weapon formed against me shall prosper"

As a child, I was beaten and whipped

I was even struck in the head

So, I wasn't gonna keep waiting around

Until they found my body cold and dead

Now I have to live with this headache

For the rest of my life

So, yeah, it was time for the revolution

Best believe I was ready to fight

So, I took my freedom

I even changed my name

I called myself Harriet Tubman

And I was about to change the game

'Cause I had a whole lotta family

Who were still being kept in the south

So, by any means necessary

I was gonna make a way out

I knew God didn't create us to be slaves

So, I became a soldier of resistance

And when folks were too scared to run

I became even more persistent

Yeah, I loved my folks
But I wasn't gon' let nobody jeopardize our mission
I said, "If you thinking about trying to go back
Somebody gonna come up missing"

"No matter what you hear or see
Don't stop; keep on running
Keep going if you want a taste of freedom
'Cause them slave catchers are coming"

So, I led them up towards north
Where Black folks could live and be free
Where they'd be far away from them slave catchers
And have a chance for happiness and liberty

That's why slave catchers were looking for me
They knew I wasn't no joke
Believe me, they knew that Harriet Tubman
Wasn't afraid to bring that smoke
See, I was manifesting the seed

That had already been planted in my mind

Yeah, I was only five feet tall

But with a pistol, I was six foot nine

They put a price on my head

And said I was wanted dead or alive

Guess you could say I was a gangster

Way ahead of my time

They made songs like "Go Down Moses"

Because the song had secret codes

Yeah, I freed about 300 folks

And I ain't never lost one soul!

I worked on the Underground Railroad

I was a proud conductor

I put my life on the line

To keep us away from those ruthless abductors

I freed my people and my family

But I wish I could have done much more

You see, it's hard to free an enslaved mind

That ain't never tasted freedom before

I did what I could for my people

And died at the age of 92

I kept doing the Lord's work

'Til there was nothing left for me to do

On my very last day

When I could feel the ancestors coming through

I looked around at my family and said

"I'm going to prepare a place for you"

I was given the name Araminta Ross

Yes, I was born a slave

But I believed we all have the right

To freedom or the grave

What they did to Black folks

Was immoral and improper

But like the Scripture says

"No weapon formed against me shall prosper!"

THE TRUTH OF SOJOURNER

Hello, Children

I was born a slave in 1797

They named me Isabella Baumfree

But way down in my spirit, I knew

That name wasn't gone be big enough for me

'Cause God was my Shepherd

And my life would not be lived in vain

So, on the day I found my purpose

"Sojourner Truth" became my name

I was taken from my family

At the precious age of nine

I was a Dutch-speaking, Black girl

Who had been sold several times

No matter who my owner was

I suffered from their physical and sexual abuse

But after my conversations with the Lord

He said, "It's time for you to run, Sojourner Truth!"

I began to walk my way to freedom

I obeyed my God's command

I became an abolitionist and preacher

And I was known throughout the land

I decided it was time for me to give my testimony

And I traveled around telling my story

I spoke about the brutality of slavery

But I gave God all the glory

I never learned to read or write

So I recounted my own tales

I was a woman chosen by God

Who simply wanted the truth to prevail

During the Civil War

I volunteered to help Union troops

I talked about the injustice we all faced

 And I was honored to be a speaker for their groups

I stood up and gave a speech

At a women's suffrage convention

I calmly asked, " Ain't I A Woman?"

And I had the whole room's attention

I once faced a mob of angry white men

They surrounded me with weapons and stones

But even they were no match for me

'Cause the power of my voice sent them home

After slaves were freed

I asked, "What about the Negroes' land?"

I even met with President Lincoln

To try and make him understand

I've always had my own opinions

And never had a problem speaking my mind

Even Frederick Douglass and I

Didn't always see eye to eye

But when all was said and done

I've done some good work over the years

And one thing folks can't say about me

Was that I lived this life in fear

'Cause I was born a slave in 1797

They named me Isabella Baumfree

But way down in my spirit, I knew

That name wasn't big enough for me

'Cause God is my Shepherd

And my life was not lived in vain

So, on the day I found my purpose

Sojourner Truth became my name!

HER NAME WAS SARAH BAARTMAN

Let me tell you about my life

This is my story from back then

They used to call me "Hottentot Venus"

And my body was grossly abused by French men

But my real name was Sarah Baartman

They say I had white folks waiting in line

To see this Khoisan African woman

Who was born with an extra-large behind

You couldn't imagine the cruelty I experienced

People paid money to see me abused

And my owners threatened to whip me

If I ever tried to refuse

They held me captive in Paris, France

They were unbelievably sick and perverse

They believed that the size of my behind

Was some kind of unnatural curse

They say my butt was so famous

That white women became jealous of my behind

And that they started making dresses

With some extra padding built inside

But I wouldn't wish that life on anyone

Being forced to be a sexual slave

Turning my body into a spectacle

Even when it was time

To lay me in my grave

But those women didn't have any compassion

Knowing that my treatment was totally inhumane

And how the white men tortured me with no remorse

'Cause they didn't have a care about my suffering and pain

So, I fought hard to keep my sanity

Despite those agonizing nights of gloom

I felt deep down in my soul

That death would be coming for me soon

I became numb to my emotions

And to the horrors in private rooms

Knowing that I would never see my home

Made me long, even more, to meet my doom

And at night when I laid down my head

Filled with trauma, misery, and pain

I hoped that one day Black women would be empowered

And that my years of suffering would not be in vain

Yet, on the last day of my life

I could still hear their voices say

"Hurry, hurry! Step right up

To see the big Black whore on stage"

Then my ancestors called me home

And I welcomed my final breath

But them folks kept my genitals and my brain

And they gave a museum in Paris the rest

Years later, Mandela sent them a letter

Telling the French, they should be ashamed

And that displaying my bones to the public

Was totally disrespectful and inhumane

That's when I was finally laid to rest

In the year of 2002

They sent my remains back to Africa

So that my bones could be entombed

Now that you know what they did

Remember my story from back then

When they used to call me "Hottentot Venus"

And my body was hatefully, brutalized by French men

A MESSAGE FROM SARAH BAARTMAN

Here's a wakeup call for Black women

And I really want y'all to hear it

Because I want all my sisters to know

That I'm still with you in spirit

Please learn the history of Sarah Baartman

'Cause I don't want your life to go to waste

Don't let anyone devalue your bodies

Sisters you don't deserve that fate

My soul is aching for today's Black women

Seems like they take pleasure in being a hottie

They don't seem to be too concerned

About advertising their precious bodies

Too many Black and brown girls go missing

Tell me, where are all the mommies?

They're getting snatched up in the streets

Like it's some kind of sport or hobby

Can't you see it's a set up?

Social media is filled with scams

They treat sexuality like a business

And a woman's body like it's her brand

It really breaks my heart to see

Black women twerking on the Gram

I bet your DMs get flooded with compliments

And countless offers for one-night stands

But I guess y'all never heard my story

So, you probably don't understand

That getting close access to Black bodies

Has always been a part of their plan

Sister, do you think you're less than royal

When you should be held above any surface?

Even if you haven't found it yet

God has already given you a purpose

Why would you degrade yourselves

And let them treat you like you're worthless?

Why do you put implants in your body

When you know it isn't worth it?

Please don't let them to exploit you

Remember what they did to me

It's been over 200 years since my death

And a lot of Black minds still aren't free

Use your minds and not your curves

To earn a living and survive

I was forced against my will

But some of y'all are selling it with pride

You have so many great choices

Allow an HBCU to educate your mind

Don't become another generation of Black women

Being pimped out like some sexual prize

That's why they don't see you as queens

The truth is you don't realize

Those kind of people will always pay money

To see the glory of a Black woman's behind!

So, let this be your wake-up call sisters

I really need you to hear it

Because I want you all to know

That I'm still with you in spirit!

THE NAME IS IDA B. WELLS

I did a lot for Black American History

I've got an important story to tell

About a poor Black girl from Memphis

Who went by the name of Ida B. Wells

I was born into slavery in 1862

But I was emancipated in 1863

Little did I know

God had some special plans for me

I had to raise my brothers and sisters

After my mamma and daddy died

But they made sure to teach us about slavery

So that their children would never be blind

But one day I was riding on a train

And a man asked me to give up my seat

I said absolutely not!

Then they dragged me off the train

And into the middle of the streets!

So, I filed a lawsuit with the courts

Because I knew that wasn't right

And later, I began writing articles about

The injustices of Black life

Although I was born in the 1800s

I was already "woke"

I wasn't gon sit around and be quiet

When we had white mobs killing Black folks

So, I spoke out about the hateful lynchings

My speeches were said to be bold

I met with prominent abolitionists

Who were glad that the truth was being told

I spoke about the injustices of Black folks

I told them that I'm not too blind to see

I said the justice you give White folks

Is not the same for folks who are Brown like me

I tirelessly fought against their twisted laws

As Black folks endured unthinkable brutality

I wanted Blacks to become more organized

So, I became a co-founder of the NAACP

I also helped to create the Alpha Suffrage Club in Chicago

To help Black women gain their equal rights

'Cause life is twice as hard for a Black woman

It's like you're instantly born with two strikes

So, I used my pen as a weapon

I became a part of a revolutionary storm

My speeches were talked about everywhere

Because I wasn't afraid to say that America was wrong!

I confronted so much violence and death threats

That I finally had to leave the South

In 1892 I moved to the city of Brooklyn

After my office space was burned out

I spoke about the corruption in law enforcement

And how there was no real justice for Blacks

I said Black folks can never get a fair trial

Because white mobs are always quick to attack

I knew American Law so well

They were like, "Who does she think she is?"

'Cause I wasn't some little terrified Black Woman

I was a Black woman who knew how to handle her biz

Yes, I've done a lot for Black American History

Mine was an important story to tell

About a poor Black girl from Memphis

Who went by the name of Ida B. Wells!

THE FREEDOM OF JUNETEENTH

Happy Juneteenth

Happy Freedom Day

The day when our people became known

As "the formerly enslaved"

Happy Jubilee

We've been "freeish" since 1865

But we didn't know the cost of freedom

Was gonna be so high

After the Emancipation Proclamation

It was the former slave owners

Who received reparations

But we were finally free

To walk away from them

Dreadful plantations

A lot of Black folks stood up

And walked off the land

I mean, it's not like Black folks

Had some kind of backup plan

And some folks went back to Africa

Yeah, they got the heck outta "Dodge"

'Cause they were tired of living in a land

Where there were no Black people in charge

Some had fought in the Civil War

For old President Abe

When that man didn't have a care

About freeing no slaves

He just wanted to preserve the Union

Of the United States

But we were contrabands of war

Who were trying to escape!

So, for a taste of freedom

We were willing to lay down our lives

Even Harriet Tubman joined in

And became a Union spy

In honor of our Black soldiers

Who were buried in unmarked graves

We treated them with dignity

By creating the first Memorial Day

Yes, we were finally "free"

Free to be lynched

Free to be defenseless and unprotected

Free to beg for food and shelter

And free to be disrespected

Folks were desperate

To find a safe place to go

So, we established Black communities

In places like Fort Monroe

You see, they gave us Freedom Day

But they also gave us Jim Crow

Freedom without a mule or land

Freedom without knowing where to go

But because of Juneteenth

We were free from the whip

Free from having our families sold

And free from the white man's grip

Then we began to dream

And that gave us some hope

But freedom didn't last too long

'Cause they started swinging that rope

As we were learning to live as free men

Others were fuming with hate

We learned real quick

That freedom didn't mean we were safe

Millions of Black folks moved north

And they called it "The Great Migration"

We created the Harlem Renaissance

That would later change the nation

And after all that we contributed

They still wouldn't leave us be

They still wanted to hold us down

And that don't sound like freedom to me

We thought freedom meant

Free to pursue opportunities

To have natural-born citizenship

And equal rights

We didn't know that freedom meant

Seeing burning crosses

On our lawns at night

We wanted to be free like Douglass!

We wanted to be free like Nat!

And we did what was necessary

To keep them lashes off our backs

We wanted to be free as a shooting star

Free as the sun going down

We wanted to be free as that man

They called Henry "Box" Brown

We wanted to be free to participate

Free to change the laws

We wanted what any man wants

We wanted to be as free as y'all

We wanted freedom of religion

Freedom of speech

Freedom of the press

And the freedom to assemble and meet

We wanted every freedom

That's been afforded to you

We wanted the right to bear arms

The same way you do

So, when we celebrate Juneteenth

We'll wear the color red

This is how we honor the ancestors

Who died and bled

And we'll eat some

Red watermelon

Red barbeque

And red velvet cake

With some red Kool -Aid

A red napkins

On a big red plate!

See, Juneteenth is about celebrating

The freedom of Blacks

Even though

They never told us

Where our forty acres was at

No, we didn't receive fair wages

Or benefits with equal pay

But after we won our freedom

Black lives changed forever that day

So, come on, Freedom

Freedom shine on thee

Freedom came at such a high cost

But the ancestors paid for you and me

So, happy Juneteenth

Happy Freedom Day

The day when our people became known

As "the formerly enslaved"

And a Happy Jubilee

We've been "freeish" since 1865

But we didn't know the cost of freedom

Was gonna be so high

THE LIGHT OF FANNIE LOU

Back in the day, when

They made it impossible for Black folks to vote

Yours truly, Fannie Lou Hamer

Was more than ready to bring that smoke

I thought, "If this is my fate

I'll be ready when it's my time

'Cause "this little light of mine

I'm gonna let it shine"

I came from a humble beginning

I lived my whole life in poverty

I felt that voting was not only a right

But the power of voting could really set us free

Yet in order for Black folks to vote

We had to know how to read

While our white counterparts walked in

Just as cool as you please

They kept us illiterate for hundreds of years

Made it illegal for us to read and write

Then when it came time for us to vote

They gave us a literacy test out of spite

To ensure their political power

Only whites were allowed to vote

And we were severely disenfranchised

And left with little to no hope

They used oppression and poll taxes

To create a system of discrimination

They used tactics like

Police power and voter intimidation

They also used terrorism

And economic retaliation

By any means necessary

They were going to control this nation

They blocked Blacks and poor whites

'Cause without money, they couldn't vote

They had to pay one to five dollars

And that was a lot for them folks

We were cursed out, beaten, and harassed

The police just didn't wanna let us pass

Today y'all walk right up to the line

But back then, Black folks couldn't even ask

White folks were the landlords

They owned the businesses and the banks

If we tried to register to vote

We would be unemployed before we could think

They retaliated against citizens

By forcing them off their land

But when it came to them white folks

They always had a plan

If this government is supposed to be,

"Of the people, by the people, and for the people"

That means it should apply to us all

Which means together we can move any mountain

No matter how big or small

We know that if the white man gives you anything

When he gets ready, he will take it right back

So, we have to fight for our freedom

Even when we're under attack

But I feel sorry for anyone

Who's wrapped up in all that hate

'Cause, how can anybody live that way

And then hope to see God's face?

So, if my strength comes from God

Then I shall not be moved

And if you think I won't succeed

Then you are a special kind of fool

Today, we are blessed to see citizens going to vote

By showing a card with their names and address

Thanks to the Voter Rights Act of 1965

Black folks don't have to deal with all that mess

'Cause back in my day

They made it impossible for Black folks to vote

But you know that

 Fannie Lou Hamer

Was more than ready to bring the smoke

So, Lord, if this be my fate

I'll be ready when it's my time

'Cause "this little light of mine

I'm gonna let it shine"

THE DAY ROSA SAT DOWN

That's right,

I agree with Sojourner, Harriet, and Ida B.

Because Black Americans have earned

The right to be proud and free

So, tell me why

Should I have to give up my seat

Yeah, my name is Rosa Parks

And you can go ahead and call the police!

No, I wasn't the first Black woman

Who refused to give up her seat on a bus

But for some reason when I did it

It created quite a big fuss

No, I didn't plan it

My actions were not premeditated

But truth be told, I was sick and tired

Of them buses being segregated

No, I wasn't old or physically tired

That's not where the problem begins
'Cause the only "tired" I was
Was that I was tired of giving in!

And, fighting for civil rights
Wasn't nothing new to me
'Cause I was already working as a secretary
Down at the NAACP

Weeks later Black folks boycotted
Those Montgomery, Alabama buses
I was put in jail for a couple of hours
But when I got out of jail
You know I was disgusted

They say because I refused to get up
Black folks started refusing to get back on the bus
And bus companies lost their customers, which was a plus
Yeah, them folks ended up losing a whole lotta bucks

Oh, but glory hallelujah
I started to hear the ancestors sing

'Cause the Montgomery Boycott was led

By a preacher named Dr. Martin Luther King

Yeah, them folks thought they had the upper hand

But they done went and messed with the wrong ones

'Cause this new Civil Rights movement

Had America on the run

And y'all know the rest

About the great Dr. King

But you see with me by his side

It was time to "let freedom ring"

So yeah, that's right,

I agree with Sojourner, Harriet, and Ida B.

Because Black Americans have earned

The right to be proud and free

So, tell me why

I won't ever have to give up my seat

Because, my name is Rosa Parks

And you can go ahead and call the police!

A POEM FOR SANDRA

My name is Sandra Bland

And yes, I left this world in pain

But all I really need right now

Is to hear you all say my name

I know that time has passed

Since they laid my body to rest

But please allow me to tell my story

To make sure that the facts are correct

Back in 2015, I began posting videos

On my Facebook page, I called it "Sandy Speaks"

I discussed topics that affected Black people

Including excessive brutality by the police

I spoke about racism and discrimination

And I spoke about the value of Black lives

And I didn't care who was offended

Because I wanted my people to survive

In 2015, I applied for job in Texas

And I was hired, which was super!

However, the next day when I drove to work

I was pulled over by a white state trooper

He said I changed lanes without signaling

But his aggressive manner left me confused

He pointed his stun gun at me so fast

That I didn't know what to do

He said that he would light me up

Apparently he saw me as some type of threat

It seems that driving while Black in Texas

Meant that I was a dangerous suspect

So, I tried to reason with the state trooper

But he just became more and more upset

He started becoming so irate

That I didn't know what was gonna happen next

My intuition was warning me inside

Because his whole vibe was suspect

As soon as I set foot out of my car

I knew that was the moment I would regret

Because he wanted to arrest me

For what was a minor traffic violation

That officer didn't have one concern

About any civil rights violation

He had intentionally escalated

That dehumanizing situation

And I ended up losing my life

Down at that corrupt police station

Because he forced me into handcuffs

And then he lied and placed me under arrest

Later they said they found me hanging in my cell

Claiming that I put that bag around my neck

But the truth is I never should have been

Locked inside that jail cell

Unfortunately, this is the sad truth

That so many Black folks still have to tell

It was tragically ironic to be in that situation

I told y'all how systemic racism was set

White folks said I was just starting trouble

But now they see Black people get no respect

Kings and Queens, that was a wake-up call

The moment my body hit the ground

'Cause anyone of us could be the next

Victim waiting to be found

And I know it was traumatic

For y'all to see my lifeless face

And for them to show my picture on the news

Was another level of disgrace

The state trooper lost his job

For committing perjury about the video tape

But for him there was one less Black American

The police would have to chase

Kings and Queens, none of us

should have to pay such a costly price

Because the police have no right

To deliberately take another person's life

And I know that if it had been anybody else

They would have put up a good fight

And I also know it wouldn't have happened

If I would have been white!

I'm so glad y'all didn't fall

For their evil twisted lies

Blaming me for my own death

And saying that this was some tragic suicide

We know that when it comes to Black skin

Lady Justice is never blind

Plus, the whole world could plainly see

What the police were trying to hide

Believe me if they did that to a queen

Who stood so righteous and tall

Then they don't plan to stop

Until they've done that to us all

But now I've become your ancestor

And my power will continue to rise

And I will still be the queen

Doing what I can to save Black lives

So, my dear Kings and Queens

I may have left this world in pain

But all I really need right now

Is to hear you say my name

WHAT IS OUR PURPOSE?

I believe that we all have a purpose

And that we're chosen for a reason

I believe that we are souls

Who have been given an opportunity

To bring about a change in this world

And the changes that we create

Will have an impact on

The souls that we touch

Sometimes we bring a lesson of joy

Sometimes we bring a lesson of sorrow

But no matter what we carry inside

There will be a lesson to teach

It is up to us to decide what we will bring

Which is where our purpose lies

Be mindful that our existence

Is about more than we know

It's way bigger than one person

A soul who understands their purpose

Will be more beneficial to this world

Than souls that think only of themselves

The blessing in our journey is this:

The more good we contribute to the world

The more we will live on in others

So, if we want to be remembered

Give the world something worth remembering

Honor and remember our ancestors

The same way you would like to be remembered

Make righteous choices

Use all of your gifts

Kick down closed doors

Break the ceiling that prevents progress

Travel the roads less traveled

And your contributions will not fade

A piece of you will always remain

The purpose inside of us will be passed on

The same we are passing on

The history of our ancestors

Is the same way that we will become

The ancestors for generations to come

And hopefully, we will have served our purpose

OTHER BOOKS BY THE AUTHOR:

Woke A Poetic Journey - 2018

Ode To The Punani: Sensual Rising - 2019

The Dream and The Lie - 2021

Tracing Black Music To The Roots - 2022

CONTACT INFORMATION:

To learn more about the author you may visit her website at Hookedonpoetry.com or you can send your inquiries to sharranctaylor00@gmail.com

SOCIAL MEDIA PAGES:

Website -   Hookedonpoetry.com

TikTok   -   @auntikween

Facebook -   @kweenyakiniauthorpage

Instagram - @kweenyakini

YouTube -   Kween Yakini's Poetry

Hashtag   -   #kweenyakini

Thank You For Reading
Telling Our Blues
With Black American Poetry

By: Sharran C. Taylor
A.K.A. Poet Kween Yakini

If You Enjoyed Reading This Book Please Leave A Review On Amazon Or Recommend It At Your Next Book Club Meeting.

www.ingramcontent.com/pod-product-compliance
Lightning Source LLC
LaVergne TN
LVHW041616070426
835507LV00008B/279